Your Simplest Life

15 UNCONVENTIONAL
TIME-MANAGEMENT SHORTCUTS:
PRODUCTIVITY TIPS AND GOAL-SETTING
TRICKS SO YOU CAN FIND TIME TO LIVE

Lisa Turner

Turner Creek

Hayesville NC

*"This wonderful book, **Your Simplest Life**, takes you by the hand and shows you how to get more done in less time than you ever thought possible. Lisa forges a path that is both unconventional and refreshing. The writing is fun, tight, and inspiring."*

March 31st, 2020 San Diego, California

—**Brian Tracy,** CEO of *Brian Tracy International,* has consulted for more than 1,000 companies, presented to more than 5 million people in more than 80 countries, and written more than 80 books.

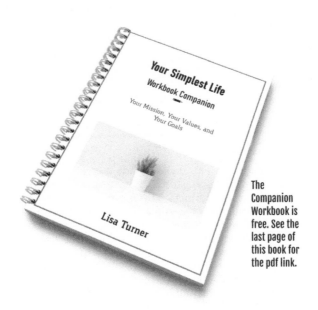

The Companion Workbook is free. See the last page of this book for the pdf link.

Lisa Turner's Other Books

iii

Note to Reader: The information, tips, and advice in this book come from the author's own education, observations, and informal research. The content provided here is for educational purposes and does not take the place of professional advice. Every effort has been made to ensure that the content is accurate and helpful for readers at publishing time. However, this is not an exhaustive treatment of the subjects. No liability is assumed for losses or damages due to the information provided. You are responsible for your own choices, actions, and results.

This book is not intended to be a substitute for the medical advice of physicians. The reader should regularly consult a physician in matters relating to his/her health, both mental and physical, and particularly with respect to any symptoms that may require diagnosis or medical attention.

Lisa Turner/Turner Creek Publishing
515 Barlow Fields Drive
Hayesville, NC 28904

See last page for link to a free companion workbook.

Your Simplest Life/ Lisa Turner —1st edition
ISBN: eBook: 978-0-9970723-6-5
ISBN: Paperback: 978-0-9970723-7-2

To Jerry

*"**Write it on** your heart that every day is the best day in the year. He is rich who owns the day, and no one owns the day who allows it to be invaded with fret and anxiety. Finish every day and be done with it. You have done what you could. Some blunders and absurdities, no doubt crept in. Forget them as soon as you can, tomorrow is a new day; begin it well and serenely, with too high a spirit to be cumbered with your old nonsense. This new day is too dear, with its hopes and invitations, to waste a moment on the yesterdays."*

—Ralph Waldo Emerson

Contents

Lisa Turner

Note to the Reader

LIFE IS NOT SIMPLE.

There are many books on the market that tell you how to be happier, how to get more done, and how to simplify your life. This book is different.

First, this book is tiny. I'm making the assumption that you chose this book because you don't want to wade through a lot of background.

Second, there is no fluff. You already have enough life experience to provide the filler.

Third, it only gives you what you need, in sectional format, so you can return to it or skip what you already know.

Fourth, I cover handling distraction, improving focus, working from home, effective planning and scheduling, attraction psychology, procrastination, time management, decluttering, values, habits, goal setting, and mindfulness – all in one small book.

Rather than being comprehensive, this book is meant to stimulate your thinking with ideas, tips, and tricks. As you feel the need for more information, go ahead and explore the paths you are interested in.

Guess what: We are not going to get everything done. But if we get the things that are important to us done, the things we care about done, we'll contribute to our own happiness, as well as the happiness of those around us.

This book is divided into three sections. The first explains how to have personal power through choice. The second shows you how to simplify your life using 15 tips and tricks. The third provides a do-it-yourself path to get what you want in life by establishing your values and then your goals.

At the end is a bonus piece of advice about getting ahead in your career. If you're still in the workplace working for someone else, this one secret can catapult you to the top of the career ladder.

To get the most out of this advice, find quiet time on your schedule to work through the exercises. Of particular importance are habits, rewards, beliefs, and values. These four areas drive up to 90 percent of your daily behavior. If you want to be more productive and less stressed/happier with what you're working on at work and at home, this time spent in self-analysis and reflection will speed you on your way.

At the end of the book is a reading list of books and articles I personally have found interesting and helpful on my own journey toward "the simplest life."

"There are no limits to what you can accomplish, except the limits you place on your own thinking."

—Brian Tracy

Introduction: Making Choices

In 1845, Henry David Thoreau retreated to solitude at Walden Pond. He wrote, "I went to the woods because I wished to live deliberately, to front only the essential facts of life, and see if I could not learn what it had to teach, and not, when I came to die, discover that I had not lived."

It is remarkable that in 1845 Thoreau thought that life could be so complicated. Imagine him thrust into today's world. He would think we were all mad.

Are we all mad?

Our phones are ringing in our pocket, our computers are beeping new email, our smart home devices are telling us our laundry is dry, the television is explaining what drugs to take and what attorneys to call after we take them. Ad jingles are circulating annoyingly in our heads. Our employers expect us to work long hours and our vacations are fleeting. It feels as if time is going faster the older we get.

Are we where we want to be right now in our lives? Are we living out a plan, or are we catch as catch can?

I'm going to argue that most of us are running full tilt from day to day, stuffing in activities and wondering where our lives are going. If you've thought this, then this book is for you. I was once there, where you might be now.

Need more time and peace of mind? Read on.

I've had a love-hate relationship with distractions. Loving the moment that I'd switch focus from what I was doing to a new track that was more fun, I'd realize that I wasn't going to get very far on the first track if I didn't drop the more exciting one and refocus. Then I'd get upset with myself. The emotions would bounce from one activity to another.

I would be proud of myself after making a detailed to-do list, only to realize 90 minutes later that I was off track. I'd patiently make another list, with a different schedule. Ninety minutes later . . . .

Humans are designed to pay attention to distractions. In the wild world, this attention protects us. If we're walking along in the jungle and hear an animal come up behind us, we pay attention, we switch focus from the path to surviving a possible attack. Our brain does this quickly, and without conscious thought. Our awareness is always tuned in to survival cues. Even when you're crossing the street and reading your email messages on your phone at the same time, your peripheral awareness is always looking for that car that is barreling toward you.

Simplify Your Life.

"Occam's razor is the problem-solving principle that states that 'Entities should not be multiplied without necessity.' The idea is attributed to English Franciscan friar William of Ockham, a scholastic philosopher and theologian." —Wikipedia

It is usually the simplest solution that works.

"Both optimists and pessimists contribute to society. The optimist invents the aeroplane, the pessimist the parachute."

—George Bernard Shaw

Section 1:
Personal Power

Earthlings rarely make choices using logic or science. Earthlings make choices using emotion and rationalization. Once you know this, you can actually modify how you choose. Using the following knowledge nuggets will help you make decisions.

While some people feel it is easier to live life going from one thing to another on a whim, this mode will not give you the concentrated time to accomplish projects and goals. In the limited amount of time that we have on this planet, why not make the most of it? My own discoveries in distraction control drove me to share this with you because of the personal benefits I'm experiencing myself. I have also found more calm and less stress in the moment in the face of adversity and more happiness and satisfaction getting the things done that I really want to do.

We all look through different filters in life. Some of the topics and opinions that I share are personal, and you may not agree with them. I hope to give you a tool or two, though, to improve your personal productivity and influence your happiness level. If I can do this for you, then I've accomplished what I set out to do.

We make decisions all the time, consciously and unconsciously, all day long. Notify your subconscious mind, which understands everything literally, that you are now going to be making choices based on the principles in this book. By doing this you will be uncovering your own personal power reserve. It's not something you need to go out and get – you already have it.

The following 11 concepts lay the foundation for maximizing your ability to make choices in the moment that will serve *you*.

The Pollyanna Principle

Begin by considering the tone of your planning. Do you approach a task assuming things will go wrong or that things will go well? Negativity, which we might think is being realistic, can be an impediment. Thinking that things will go wrong can become a self-fulfilling prophecy. If you worry ahead of events so you'll be "prepared" in case something goes wrong turns into endless scenarios. And if something does go wrong, it's usually not the thing that you worried about.

This runs in both directions, of course. I'm the Pollyanna type, and chronically underestimate how long a task will take, from changing the oil in the airplane to cleaning out the closet. I'd assume the best of everyone in every situation and skip the critical thinking that would lead to the best decisions.

But if you have to pick between the two, pick the positive.

The way the Pollyanna principle works is to really appreciate when things are going well, and make the best of things when they are going poorly. I'm not saying to not face reality, but to maneuver your own reactions to the positive side. Perception is everything. Over time, this can become a habit. It will be difficult at first, but persevere. In a *New York Times* Smarter Living article, columnist Tim Herrera noted that "worrying about when the other shoe will drop will only steal your current joy."

Think about what you want, even if you're not sure right now. In the third Section of this book we'll talk in detail about discovering what you care about, the things you enjoy, and the dreams that you have.

"Pollyanna thinking" means the internal dialogue and pictures sync with a positive view of yourself rather than thinking about what you don't want or what you worry about. This is also a key concept in the Law of Attraction principles.

Belief Systems

The power of perception and the resulting beliefs drive what we do every day. Beliefs are perhaps the most powerful determinants of human behavior there is. A person or a group can become so entrenched in a belief that they become blind and irrational.

We acquire our belief systems while growing up, as we observe others around us. Because they are emotionally powerful and reinforcing, it's difficult to change them. It may be easier to add a belief rather than change an existing belief.

If we are going to change how we do things day to day — for example, not watching the TV after dinner — then we will need to change how we view these habits, and *believe* that there is a better way to arrange our time.

In the third Section of this book I will talk about discovering your own values and how to base goals upon them. Values are tied closely to beliefs. Most of us haven't even thought about what our values are. If you find this fascinating, consider reading *Sapiens: A Brief History of Mankind*, by Yuval Harari.

Habit Recognition

Habits are so ingrained into our daily lives we rarely think about them. But recognizing our habits and doing a little bit of self-reflection can make an enormous difference in our level of productivity. If we have a habit of watching TV right after dinner for three hours, and we decide to make that two hours and use that extra hour for a walk, a project, or reading, we've made a big change. This is why I keep saying that *personal choice* in what we do is so critical.

One simple exercise you can do is spend an hour alone at your desk and write out all of your habits. Use one side of the paper for what you consider to be good habits, and the other side for what you consider to be bad habits. Or, you can use two notebooks. You will remember more if you take several sessions to do this exercise.

Are you surprised? We're habit driven creatures. Another self-protection feature, habits are designed so that we are close to mindless when we do them. Have you ever driven down the road to work and then forgotten driving the route? It's a great example of a habit where we're working on other problems in our head. Our subconscious is still looking for danger even though we don't remember paying attention.

What habits would you like to change? Most people say the habits around eating, spending, and personal relationships. Changing habits can be surprisingly difficult. My advice is to pick one at a time, and do some analysis on it before you begin. What drives the habit? When do you do it? What's your reasoning? What are the cues that drive your good habits? Can you use any of the same reasoning with your bad habits?

Most of us choose to replace a bad habit with a new habit that is too ambitious. This is like a 100-percent change — from bad to good — and it's easy to fail. Failure reinforces the old behavior, so we must approach it a different way. After doing the habit recognition exercise, write out a few things that you want to change. Start very small, and reward yourself.

Habits are propagated by rewards in a circular, reinforcing pattern. Identify the good habits and the rewards. Then the poor habits and the "rewards." Pick out one small, "bad" habit. Why is it a bad habit? Could you change it? If you pick it apart and identify the trigger, the response, and the reward, you can substitute other actions to get a better result. Returning to the example above where we talked about three hours of TV after dinner – you can trade some of that time for something else, but it has to have a reward that's as good as the TV watching. Analyze the trade. Pick out a reward that's bigger, and install a new habit.

James Clear, the author of *Atomic Habits*, explodes the myth that if you repeat the habit for 21 days you're set. Clear says 66 days. My advice is START with 21 and keep going. Every time you repeat a new pattern of behavior, it reinforces the brain's ability to recognize it. The reinforcement gets stronger with every repeat. A key thing to remember is that both good and bad habits tend to be "mindless" – in other words, we're not doing them consciously. The more conscious you are, the more successful you will be in installing new habits. We'll be talking about how to be more mindful later in the book.

Another reinforcing trick to consider in good habit formation is using hypnosis training. Hypnotherapy works particularly well for habit modification. At the end of the book you'll find information on where to look for what I consider to be the best programs. They are inexpensive (some are free) and cover just about any habit you'd like to change. After going through the training, you can even record your own script targeting what you want to work on. I've tried this myself and have found it to be very effective. I'll talk more about hypnosis in the next Section.

Master Distractions

Understanding the power of choice is critical to staying on a task or doing something else. Responding to distraction consists of quick, tiny habits that we need to recognize before we can do anything about them. The actions and the rewards are very close together, which make them powerful. In Section II I'll show you how to recognize and deal with them. Reducing distraction is all about where we place our attention.

The management of distraction is two-pronged. The first is to create time blocks, or compartments, that allow you to do concentrated, focused work; the second are the techniques we will talk about to create those compartments. Once created, you will find it much easier to conduct what some psychologists call "deep work," or work that is totally focused and 100 percent free of distraction. This is a choice you make; not all work needs this protection.

Compartmentalizing tricks follow in Section II.

The Law of Accumulation

Isn't it odd that if you don't have a lot of stuff, it will diminish, but if you have a lot of stuff it grows. The Law of Closets says that the more closets you have, the fuller they will each be. Of course, I am making these up, but it does feel as if things tend to accumulate over time.

Another psychological oddity we should recognize is what I call the Law of Small Numbers. I'll bet you have online subscriptions to things that pop up every month. "Ah, that's only $1.99 a month. I'm not going to worry about it," you say. Except that if you add up all of those subscriptions, you might discover that they are $75 a month. That's a lot of money. Suddenly the deals don't look so great.

What to do? Just like your junk drawer, which we'll take about later, make sure you need and are using all of your subscriptions and the "little stuff," because it adds up. And over time you might feel that they are consuming a lot of your attention. Should they be?

You may have also noticed that getting on email lists propagates exponentially. You download a free book and now you're on another list; you request information and now you're on yet another list. When you open your email you see it clogged with all of these newsletters, newspaper columns, subscriptions, and info letters you thought you'd read every day. My point is that you may be spending a lot of time wading through email when you should really be making finer choices about the time you're giving up to read all of these information newsletters and stories.

Regrets

Anything in your life that you regret so far? Of course there is. I'll guess that there are lots of things that have happened in the past that bother you. There are for me. These regrets are emotionally charged and tend to follow you around. We can harbor regret about something that happened a long time ago, even when others have forgotten all about it. Once again, our perception can be that the offense, or the remark, or the snub is still fresh with others because it may be for us.

The key to making regret evaporate is realizing that we cannot do any more than we already have in correcting it or making it go away. The more we push it, the bigger it gets. It's like a monster that keeps reappearing after we think we've closed and locked the door.

The second thing we can do is open the door and take a really good look at our monsters. List them out if that helps, or talk to a trusted friend. Then decide what you would do differently if faced with the same situation now.

Learn from it. Play that out in your mind. Now let it go.

The third thing you can do is forgive *yourself*. You don't have to like what someone else did, or what you did, but investing time in experiencing pain inside yourself will only amplify it.

Baggage

We all have "stuff" that we're carrying around emotionally. Most of it attached itself to us when we were children, when we suffered in a variety of ways or experienced trauma that stuck with us. I'm not a psychiatrist and am not in a position to diagnose these problems, but I can say that most of us have some emotionally charged experiences that we've carried with us our whole life. They usually involve relationships and fears that we had when we were young, and we carry them into adulthood.

Mind space, or "emotional decluttering," can be so complicated that therapies have been developed to address it. From professional psychotherapy to a host of self-help books, it's a problem that many people find deeply troubling. There's no single best path out, except to say that recognizing what I call "emotional baggage" is a start in figuring out how to feel better.

If you have deeply held "stuff" and it affects your life now, then stop reading this and get help. This book does not substitute for medical advice.

If you're functional and have mastered most of these early traumas, I am guessing that you might still have some "baggage" that you are carrying around. This "stuff" includes blaming others for things that happened to you, relying on excuses to explain why you do things a certain way, or just general guilt or regrets about things that happened.

Recognize that most of us are carrying these "bags" around with us wherever we go. This is really a drag on our performance and happiness in the moment. What to do? When you get upset over something, ask yourself if it's a current concern or one that you're carrying around. If you recognize you're carrying things, try to drop them. At least put them in a storage shed.

If you're troubled thinking about this, consider getting your notebook out and writing down a list of "bags" you think you're carrying. Write down why you think you're holding on to each one. Let the list sit for a day or two and then return to it. Your subconscious mind will be figuring it out and when you return to the list you may find answers waiting. Can you let it go?

Don't take other people's bags. Certainly, help them if they need help, but don't take their bags home with you. They will ask. Say no.

The Boredom Signal

Feeling bored with your activities is a signal that you need to change gears and do something else. A lack of choice or control can drive this feeling, as can a feeling that you want to avoid an activity because you're uncomfortable with it. Feeling bored can also be a signal that you've lost interest in essential life activities.

If you're feeling bored, take a moment to write down why. Be honest with yourself. If you're feeling depressed, take stock of how low you feel; you may need to get some help from a professional.

The ordinary boredom we sometimes experience can best be handled by a brief internal analysis and then switching gears to something else that you enjoy. When energy returns, you can get back on the tasks you were doing. Everything in life runs on its own cycle; sometimes we need to just wait for the uptick.

Acceptance

Bill Harris, director of the Centerpointe Research Institute, wrote a wonderful article called *Nine Principles for Conscious Living* in 2007. In it he states "Let whatever happens be okay." This is not his version of floppy living where you don't give a damn. This is his version of being serious about freeing yourself from your misconceptions. Most of us don't realize that we have the choice to decide how we're going to feel about something. He is saying to not get attached to what we want, because we're not always going to get what we want. It doesn't mean we can't take action to change a situation; it only means that we should accept it first. Try this the next time you find yourself annoyed at something that's out of your control.

The Pollyanna Principle works well here. Life is going to throw nasty surprises our way along with the good stuff. The nasty things can get us down, get us depressed, get us wondering why this happened to us. Descending into negativity will only make it harder to recover from an emotional or physical shock. When people ask me why I'm so positive, I say, "Consider the alternative." You have the choice to decide how you are going to feel about something. Staying positive and taking the best out of where you find yourself will nearly always improve the situation, if not at least your own reaction to it.

You'll surprise the people around you as well as yourself the next time you practice this reaction. It's important to note that making the best of a bad situation does not obviate a serious response or critical thinking.

Self-Mastery

Self-mastery or self-discipline means exercising the power of choice in choosing for the future rather than choosing the easiest thing in the moment. It does not mean "self-punishment," although it may feel like it when you get up early to work out.

Exercising self-discipline is the expression of big picture, long-term thinking, understanding the consequences of actions, and doing the things that are right, according to your values.

Foregoing instant gratification and pleasure for a greater reward later in spite of inconvenience, hardship, and difficulty will build our ability to meet our goals long term.

Just because the path of least resistance is easier doesn't mean it's the best course of action. To get to a point of self-mastery, you'll need to exercise conscious awareness combined with a long-range view of what results you want. Develop this as a habit, and the rewards will drive both self-esteem and personal power.

The best way to engage the power of self-discipline is to focus on small commitments and build up to bigger ones, just as you would if you were building a physical exercise program.

Brian Tracy, a well-known author of more than 80 bestselling books, has contributed more to the field of self-mastery than any other coach on the planet. I recommend his books if you want to learn more about the techniques.

Me Time

It's okay! Cool it, chill, relax. If you're feeling timid, shy, uncertain, and overwhelmed, remember that we're all suffering in life periodically. No matter how hard you try, there will be times when you're just not having a good day. To be human means dealing with problems.

You already know that being available all of the time to everyone creates stress and fatigue. But how do you manage this stress? We've been raised with computers, cell phones, smart speakers, apps and notifications that are competing for our attention, and smart video boxes that are supposed to be able to answer science questions but quickly get confused.

Trick: Imagine a bubble around yourself that you can turn on and off. A cloak, if you will. Decide when on your schedule you will "cloak." Generally speaking, you unplugging yourself from the world for an hour or two will not result in the planet imploding. We'll talk more about this in the next Section.

"You don't run out of time; you run out of attention."

—Lisa Turner

◼▶

Section II: Tips & Tricks

It's not the when or the why. We know the when and the why. It's the how.

"Don't do it that way."

"Don't feel bad."

"Get a grip."

All easy to say, but *how* do we exercise the principles, *how* do we become more focused, *how* do we become happier, and *how* can we obtain more inner peace? In this section I'll give you 15 tips to do just that. Even if only a few work for you, you'll be farther ahead and get more done. Return to the book after you've mastered a few of these, and take a look at doing some more.

What's so tough about being distracted? Linda Stone, a former Apple and Microsoft executive, calls continuous partial attention, or "CPA," a "state of alertness during which you are motivated by the desire to not miss out on anything." If you're a 70-year-old, you may not recognize this, but if you're a millennial parent or a teenager, you know exactly what this condition looks and feels like.

Lots of distractions add up to higher stress levels and more fatigue. Most importantly, they can prevent us from being highly productive and prevent us from feeling good about what we're accomplishing. We feel that we're not getting enough done.

This distraction trap has been in the making for a long time. When I first started my corporate career in management, I was given a beeper. Not sure what a beeper is? It was a little square electronic box meant to be attached to your belt that your boss could trigger so that he or she could have you call them immediately. Pretty odd, huh?

You could choose to ignore it at your peril, pretending that the "signal" didn't go through. This always worked well when you were on an extended lunch break shopping in a mall or had to run home for a special tryst with your boyfriend.

As archaic as it sounds, it is so much worse now, because we have few excuses about being unreachable. We also have a lot more beeping and alerting gadgets on our desks, in our pockets, and on our wrists.

What can we do? Plenty. Read on.

"The only reason for time is so that every-thing doesn't happen at once."

—Albert Einstein

Communications and Social Media

This can be simplified by understanding how complicated it is.

Generationally we have three sets of issues. Those born prior to 1946 who did not grow up with electronics and who didn't get the "tech gene" can, and do, choose to ignore such distractions. This group doesn't understand the rest of us in terms of communications availability and variety, and they really aren't concerned about it.

The middle group – Gen-X and Baby Boomers, born from 1946 to 1979 – is conflicted. They want to use tech but also want to dismiss it as being "too much" or "complicated." If you quiz people on the street from these generations, they will either aspire to Millennial tech savvy or they will dismiss it as being unnecessary. Talk about complicated!

Those born after 1979 – Millennials or Gen Y and the latest Gen Z – have been raised with computers, cell phones, smart speakers, cars that talk to them, cameras that talk to them, and a real sense that they should be responding real time to all of these demands. Not only do they see these things as normal, they wonder why the devices are not smarter than they are.

This group also takes tech for granted. A home with no Internet? No way! Electricity, electronic devices, and wireless communications have always been around, right?

The American Psychological Association performed an extensive survey in 2017 about electronic devices and stress. Unsurprisingly, the headline reads: "APA's Survey Finds Constantly Checking Electronic Devices Linked to Significant Stress for Most Americans."[1]

Some people are so attached to instant communications that they can't put their phone away for 30 minutes. Are you one of them? If you are, then this goes in the stressful habit column, which we will talk about later. Think it through – do you really need to be available at all hours of the day and night? Why not trade this residual stress for a compartmentalized schedule where you can choose when you're available? Will the world self-destruct?

In Section I we talked about the power of choice. It's the most powerful tool you have to make decisions about what you'll allow into your distraction zone and what you'll keep out.

---

[1] American Psychological Association (apa.org) website news article: *APA's Survey Finds Constantly Checking Electronic Devices Linked to Significant Stress for Most Americans,* February 23, 2017.
https://www.apa.org/news/press/releases/2017/02/chec king-devices

Phone and Media: Availability

Actively decide when you'll answer your phone and be available through Messenger, Snapchat, WhatsApp, and other messaging services. They can be insidious, pervasive, and addicting. Even if you don't get a lot of messaging from others, just one message thread can get you off track if you're working on something important.

Moving into this space recently are group video apps, like HouseParty and Airtime. As a virtual group get-together, these apps can suck up a lot of time.

If you get calls all the time, it's even more important to control when you'll be available. If everyone is trained to know you are always going to answer, then you need to change this by letting them know that you've changed your habits and you'll be "turning off" for compartmentalized work. This way, they won't feel slighted if you don't respond immediately.

Learn how to compartmentalize. You can do this mentally by determining how much time you need to accomplish something important, and then sealing off the outside world. Do this by locating your phone in another place or turning on the do-not-disturb option.

Think about the times you've become immersed in something you love. It could be painting, walking a path, reading, or anything that focuses you on the experience. (In brain research this is called the Flow State. The flow state is activated when the alpha and theta brain waves meet – this is the border between the conscious and subconscious mind.) For really deep-thinking projects, this state will give you enormous focusing ability as well as creative power.

Distractions are big interrupters when you are "in the flow." Think about reading a fascinating book with a single light shining on the page, and then the light suddenly goes out. In surprise, your brain switches to survival mode. Getting back into the flow is not like a light switch, and you'll spend some time getting back to it. The residual effects from the surprise (be it a phone ringing, an alert, or a notification) will linger, and it will be difficult to get back on track.

To compartmentalize your time, imagine a bubble around yourself that you can turn on and off.

How: Find a quiet place to retreat to, or put your noise-cancelling headphones on. At work, use some kind of signal to others that you are working on a project and cannot be disturbed. Imagine a protective capsule or cloak around you and your work space. As you practice this technique you will get better at it.

Exceptions: If there's an emergency of some sort going on in your life, make yourself fully available. But this should not be an everyday occurrence. Even if you are a caretaker for another person, you need to make some pockets of time for yourself.

TV, Radio, and Music

When I was growing up there was a single TV in the house. If the TV was on, there were people actively watching it. Now the TV has taken the place of radio; it's on much of the time, and half the time no one is watching it.

I used to have a subscription to DirecTV Sunday Ticket. I'd put on the screen with eight picture-in-picture games going all at once. I'd sit down at my desk and start working on something. About every four minutes I'd jump up and run over to the big screen and watch for five minutes. Then back to my desk. How much do you think I got done? Nothing. Not only that, I was frustrated watching all eight games at the same time. Switching back and forth between games didn't help. Finally, I decided on one game — coincidentally the game that was broadcast locally — and enjoyed watching it. The following year I dropped Sunday Ticket. I still miss it, but I'm glad I don't have it.

Driven by profiteers, the "facts" in TV commercials are rarely questioned, but they should be. Marketing has gotten so sophisticated; we're led to believe that all the assertions are true. Marketing power, driven by money and psychological research, make what you're watching and hearing very appealing. Who wouldn't want to have fewer wrinkles and more brainpower? The trouble is that we're spending precious hours of our life watching and listening to things that just aren't true.

TV commercials can be corrosive. They tell your subconscious that things are not okay the way they are. They tell you that you need something. You actually rarely need what they are selling, and if you do need something, there are much better ways of finding what you need than taking the advice from a commercial. If you are intrigued by something, try to decode the pitch and then research it. You can almost always find the product for less money somewhere else.

What's more insidious is when we fall asleep in front of the TV. Marketers understand their audience, so if subliminal programming does work, they are going to be selling a lot of what they are advertising to sleeping people.

Actively manage TV programming. The way to do this is to choose what you want to watch, and mute the commercials. Don't listen to the

TV unless you're actively watching something you're interested in, and even then, have your remote control handy and turn off the sound when commercial breaks come on. You'll have to do it fast, because the marketers know they have to catch you quickly with quirky images and sounds.

HOW: All modern TVs have remotes. Find a red sharpie and draw a bold circle around the MUTE key. Why these keys aren't twice as big as all the others and put in a prominent position on the device is a mystery to me. We've all looked for this key in a panic at times, overlooking it.

Turn the sound off during a commercial break. Even better, use your DVR to record everything you like, and skip over the commercials when you're watching. Once you begin doing this, you will realize how incredibly annoying commercials are and how much stress seems to lift when you have so much control.

Exceptions. There is one exception to this rule. It's called the Super Bowl. The Super Bowl is a showcase for new commercials, and as such can be a lot of fun. Just don't fall asleep.

Other exceptions. Yes, there are people who seem to be able to blot out all sound distractions. I'm going to propose that these TV sounds are still going to invade your brain as potential subliminal interference, or noise. But if you're fine with it, so am I.

Working from Home

Working from your home can be an absolute joy. It offers the ability to control distractions and schedule. But working at home is not for everybody. If it's right for you, you will know it in the first week you try it. If it's not for you, you'll experience swings in concentration in the first few days and discover lots of distractions.

If working at home is thrust upon you, as it was in the most recent global virus pandemic, then you can choose to discover its benefits. I emphasize choose, because resistance on your part will only make you more miserable.

Re-read the first section in this book on personal choice and the Pollyanna principle. Along with a mindfulness practice, you have the power to recognize when a change in habits and circumstances can upend your comfort levels.

Just as any life-changing event can be tough to handle, resolve to make the best of the situation. Keys for getting comfortable and productive working at home include three rules.

The first rule is to find a space — any space — where you have privacy and can control sound. This should include noise-canceling headphones or earbuds if you need them. The privacy will allow you to plan and arrange your work, and control your distractions. This space becomes your territory when you "go to work" and the rest of the family needs to understand this. It's not easy – but it's important.

The second rule is arranging breaks every 60 to 90 minutes. This may seem like a lot, but humans have relatively short attention spans, and productivity will give way to distraction sooner rather than later without breaks. Make your social interactions planned, if you can, rather than allowing lots of interruptions. Taking a 10-minute break every hour allows you to catch up on some of these other demands. It also gives you some physical release.

The third rule is to build free time into your work, home, and play schedule. If you're an over-achiever and you start working from home, you will be working all of the time and wonder why you're feeling overwhelmed. This is especially true if you have a family at home with you. The way to solve the problem is to compartmentalize your time schedule (which I'll talk about later in this Section), and communicate the schedule to others so that they will be less resentful when you can't respond to them immediately.

Consider building in an entire "free day" into your schedule every four or five days. By definition, this is time that you can use to catch up, or go play and not feel guilty.

Music: Pay Attention . . . or Not

Like TV, actively manage what you're listening to. Recognize that the amount of concentration you need and how much music might interfere with what you're doing depends entirely on what you're doing. When working out or walking/running, it can be helpful, but while reading or writing it can slow you down. There will be times when complete quiet when driving your car will help concentration and allow you to do planning.

If you're comfortable driving and listening to media, then one great way to enrich yourself is through podcasts, self-improvement programs, and educational programs. If you find yourself turning down the volume during the drive because of traffic, this is a signal to turn it off until you've navigated the difficult areas.

Hypnosis and Affirmations

Hypnosis has been around since the 17th century. Does it work? If you believe it does, yes. Rather than a wishy-washy answer, this is a reflection on the nature of both hypnosis and affirmations; belief is everything. I said earlier that one of the most powerful determinants of our behavior is our beliefs. Both hypnosis, or suggestions delivered when you are in a relaxed state, and affirmations — deliberate positive statements delivered in a relaxed state — can be powerful in rewiring habits and thinking patterns.

I recommend hypnotherapy programs for helping you reprogram your brain (subconscious mind) for changing old habits and instilling new habits. I've listed one source in the resources list at the end of this book. Your investment will be one of time rather than money with most hypnosis audio programs or books. Many are free; but you will need to commit to listening to the programs and following up to make sure the changes are reinforced.

Sound Therapy

Another category of sound and its impact on focus and health is called sound therapy, sound healing, or sound meditation. The use of specific music, beats, or sounds can be used for a variety of purposes and are usually overseen by a trained practitioner. *Healing Music Organization* in Santa Cruz, California, is one of the more known resources for information on programs and practitioners in the United States.

You've already utilized "sound therapy" if you've ever listened to waterfalls or white noise going to sleep.

If you're using sound therapy, follow the instructions, which will usually involve a focused session rather than doing other things at the same time.

Like hypnotherapy and meditation, doing other things while listening will prevent you from getting the full benefit of the therapy, and in some cases — driving for example — may be dangerous while listening to a therapeutic program meant to engage your full attention.

One therapy that has become very popular over the last several decades is brainwave entrainment. Soundtracks can be made to elicit specific brain-wave patterns. Producing any of the five known brainwave patterns – Delta, Alpha, Beta, Theta, and Gamma — can drive specific results, from inducing sleep and relaxation to entering very deep meditative states.

A technique called binaural beats — listening to different audio frequencies in each ear — was used as early as 1839, and has progressed to some very sophisticated technology to induce sleep, meditation, and other brain states. One well-known provider in this space is Centerpointe Research Institute with their progressive product called Holosync.[2] Centerpointe users say the programs helped them enter meditative states more quickly and more deeply.

If you are using specific sound therapy, use it with the directions to get the maximum benefit.

Headphones and Noise-Reducing Technology

It may be particularly difficult in our modern world to find any peace and quiet. Enter sound and noise control by using headphones, earplugs, or noise-canceling earbuds. Controlling noise and sound can reduce stress and improve focus. On the other end of the spectrum — if you have trouble hearing — consider hearing aids in the form of sound amplification or professional hearing devices. Do your research, because hearing aids have been deregulated from their status as medical devices, so prices should be more reasonable in the future.

If you use hypnotherapy or if you meditate, I recommend the use of headphones or noise-cancelling earbuds.

Tip: Can't get a jingle out of your head? Listen to a song you like several times through, singing along. The other tune will fade away. Maybe.

---

[2] See the resources list at the end of the book for information on Centerpointe programs.

Multi-Tasking

This subject ties in with the items above but deserves its own rule.

Multi-tasking is focusing on more than one thing at the same time. Psychologists say that a person can't do two or more things at one time effectively. This is a generalization that depends on what you are doing.

If you are a concert pianist playing in City Hall, you're doing a lot of things simultaneously, and doing them well. Your hands and your feet are receiving instructions from your brain, you're reading music, and you're thinking about the audience and your music pacing.

If you're writing a novel and you're in the middle of an exciting action sequence and your email beeps, should you switch gears and look at the email? You can, but there will be a focus penalty. As much as you think you can switch gears back to what you were doing, it's going to remove some of the horsepower while you're dealing with the email. Think of this as bicycling uphill. You're writing your book, flying along, and then your email beeps. Now you slowing, hitting a steep slope, and it's taking more energy to cycle. You'll spend another 15 minutes dealing with the interruption and then trying to figure out where you were.

Make time compartments for "deep work" and turn off all alerts, knowing you'll come out the other side having accomplished what you needed to do and, amazingly, the world didn't end.

Multi-Tasking and Attention

There's nothing wrong with multi-tasking as long as you understand that it's going to take longer to accomplish the primary mission. It's up to you. My advice is to make the decision before you begin something important. Give yourself breaks from intense work, and catch up on calls and mail then.

Remember that where you place your attention is your choice. Figure out what things need protected time.

What about switching gears while you're in the middle of something else? For example, you're putting the laundry into the dryer and you realize that the latch is sticky. You make a mental note to write down "lubricate the latch on the dryer." Why not just go and grab the spray grease from the kitchen right now? Go for it! There's nothing wrong with this multi-tasking. In fact, you just saved yourself one more item on your tiny to-dos.

One caution on quick-thought multi-tasking though: Be attentive and focused as you switch gears. Have you ever ended up in a room only to wonder why you were there?

Procrastination

Society views habitual procrastinators as individuals who have no discipline, are poor planners, and don't care about time. While there may be extremes, this view is misguided. Most of us "procrastinate" or put things off, and it's often for a good reason.

I'd prefer to call procrastination "delaying a decision." When we put something off it's because:

- ✓ We're not sure we want to do it at all;
- ✓ We don't know where to begin;
- ✓ It triggers something bad from a previous experience that causes us to resist it;
- ✓ We fear failure if we start.

These are protective behaviors caused by our subconscious, and if we don't recognize them, then we won't get out of the trap.

If this is a habitual problem for you, then come to terms with it rather than finding something else to blame. In the analysis of our own thinking patterns, we will realize what the fear is, and this will help us to overcome it.

You may find that the delay in action brings a positive result. You may discover a better way to proceed, you may realize that delegating the task or project would yield a better outcome, or you may realize that it didn't even need to be done. The key is to take the time to find out why you're resisting by thinking it all the way through. Then make the decision about what you're going to do.

Planning and Scheduling/To-Do Lists

After studying productivity in the workplace for most of my career, I've always been obsessed with planning and maximizing what I get done personally. For years I would make lists of what I needed to get done, and for years I would underestimate how long something would take. Sometimes I would get so frustrated I would tear up the planning sheet and start completely over – wasting even more time.

Off the top of my head I'd make a list of things I had to do for the week. I'd coordinate it with my calendar so I wouldn't forget anything.

I'd estimate how long something would take, and how important it was. In spite of all this careful and judicious scheduling, I'd nearly always underestimate the time I needed, and I'd underestimate the number of distractions and "jump-the-line" things that would intrude.

You'd think that year over year I'd learn something from these failures. But I'd keep trying "harder" and think that would improve my methods. I attributed my inability to plan to my Type A "Let's do everything right now" personality. I'd accepted routine failures at raising my productivity when in the back of my mind I knew I could do better.

Then I had a breakthrough.

In 1996 I started building a kit airplane in my garage. It was a massive project. I also worked full time in management at a corporation 30 minutes away. Working in management means working at least 60 hours a week, and although I enjoyed it, it was a job full of time-consuming, detailed, and often-difficult tasks.

How would I use my free time at night and on the weekends to build the airplane?

A decade earlier I had been challenged with working during the day and attending night school for my masters and doctoral degrees. It was only by not having a family to raise that I was able to fit everything in. The experience put me in absolute awe of people who are raising children, working, and going to school at the same time.

I realized that the situation with the airplane was different from night school, because I wanted to spend every waking moment on the airplane. Faced with logistics that seemed impossible, I did something radical: I planned a lot of extra time into my build schedule. Rather than tightening it up, as you might expect, I relaxed it. And I got very detailed in my plan.

What happened? I got everything done, and I was ahead of my schedule on most days. I can't explain how refreshing this was. It completely changed how I plan.

I'd like to share it with you. Just realize that we're all different, and there are dozens of planning systems out there that work. What I'm about to share goes completely against the grain of most planning systems in books today.

Getting the Right Things Done

Carry a pen or pencil and paper around with you. It can be a folded sheet in your pocket or you can get fancy and have a small notepad. But carry something every day. When you think of things to put on your list, write it down. If you prefer the digital life, that works too. Just remember to retrieve your voice memos at the end of the day. I know that paper and pencil is old-fashioned, but it's available, doesn't need electricity or a phone, and works.

Have a calendar. Once again, you can use digital calendars. I personally prefer paper I can look at, but that's how I grew up, so I like that. I have several calendars, and I plan different parts of my life on different calendars. You can have one for work, one for home projects, one for building your airplane or whatever your big project is.

Compartmentalize if you enjoy routine. For example, every Wednesday from 7 pm to 9 pm you're going to write in your journal, listen to a podcast, work on your airplane, etc. It's essentially free time that you designate, depending upon the priorities you establish with your to-do lists.

Don't beat up on yourself when you don't get everything done, or some days even half of the things done. That stress just adds to upset. You need to factor in the "human" part of life, realizing that we are going to have calamities and shifts and we need to respond with flexibility. This was one lesson it took me a long time to learn. I just kept trying to fit a quart of water into a cup and it never, ever worked. If you are a high achiever you will rail against this advice, but in the end the acceptance that we just don't have control over the whole mess is liberating.

Start out by doing a to-do dump on a sheet of notepaper. It may take several pages. Just list out everything you can think of. Make your own categories, or use mine. I use <u>this month</u>, <u>this year</u>, <u>next five years</u>. As you move out on the timeline, everything you're putting down gets much more general, of course. You'll have a dozen or more things for this month, perhaps a dozen things this year, and as few as three to six things for the five-year block. That five-year block is for things such as get a master's degree, travel to Spain, build a house, start a family, write a book, learn the piano. The long-range things will stay in your brain if you don't plan them and start them sometime.

You should start with the five-year block and work back. You should find this exercise to be fun and creative; if you really get going on it, consider skipping ahead to the last Section of this book on goal setting and then returning here.

So now you have your lists. The one-year list and the five-year list will stay at the ready in your notebook or with your calendar. Feel free to add to them. What you want to spend time on now is your month list. You may enjoy a daily journal sort of calendar, week-at-a-glance, or a month-at-a-glance.

Take the month list and your calendar. Where's your free time? Block out the areas where you have other commitments. Using pencil, I draw sections on the calendar where I can do whatever I want.

Now look at the list. Because it's a month, it's more high level than your week list is going to be, and gives you a sense for what you have to get accomplished. Realize that if you work in the other direction – from the day in front of you up to the week and month – you may miss the larger items.

Let's say you have 15 things on your month list, from change the oil in the lawn tractor to clean out the closets. You'll have have-to-do items and nice-to-do items, and, hopefully, you'll have be-nice-to-me items like watching a movie, taking a trip, reading, etc. If there are any must-do-at-a-certain-time items, like getting ready for company, load these into your calendar and assign a time. Then add either 30 percent or even 50 percent more time than you think you need.

I hear you. "I can't lengthen the time because I won't get it done." Okay then. If you're really good at time estimates (I am not), then don't add the time. But when you run out of time, I told you so!

Now to the essential pieces of to-do lists. What I'm about to tell you is the flywheel, or power driver, behind being successful at getting things done with your lists.

Planning your week and your day start with a review of your year and month lists. Make sure you're not missing something; add things you think of, and make sure the priorities are where you want them. This review will take you all of two minutes.

Now look at your week. How will you break items down? When I was working on the airplane, I dedicated a block of time ahead of every week to list out the specific tasks I had to accomplish based on the instructions and plans that came with the kit. I actually penciled in times next to the items and then added a factor of 30 percent. I also did this with the mundane, have-to-do items like cleaning the house, grocery shopping, mowing the lawn, etc. As long as I added the extra time, the schedule ran well and I was pleased with progress.

The success of your daily list now flows from your week's analysis. Just remember that even after you've broken your task list down into pieces, be careful not to underestimate the time things will take. Look at it this way: When you finish something early you can give yourself a pat on the back and launch into something else.

This advice is at odds with many time management experts who say to be realistic about the time things take. I just don't believe in our overfull world of activities that this works well, and when we fall behind, we tend to get upset with ourselves.

Assemble your daily list the night before, or in the morning. Put the tiny mundane things off to the side in their own section. This includes quick phone calls, taking out the trash, sending a quick email. While you don't want to forget these things, they are not the main list items.

One trick with your weekly schedule is to use tiny Post-It notes (or make your own) to list the week's items and then you can move them around on your calendar. You can also assign priority based on color. If you're a visual person you might find this useful. Or, you can use apps like Trello, Todoist, or Kanban Flow. I use the top half of sticky notes, labeled and cut to a small size, to move to-dos around on my calendar. It beats pulling out the Wite-Out®. One sticky note will give me three movables.

Back to your daily list. Pick two or three things that you can commit to. How long will they take? What is the priority order? Do any of these tasks need to be broken down further? Realize also that the things you tackle first are more likely to get done.

Some folks like the Stephen Covey method of important-not important vs. urgent-not urgent. Covey wrote *The 7 Habits of Highly Effective People* in 1989, and it remains a bestseller on self-management. Personally, I don't like the method, because I believe we intuitively assign these values to our items and I don't like over-analyzing the list. Covey's charts are complex and, in my opinion, not likely to be used in real life. The longer we have to mess around with where things go on the list the less likely we are to even do a list. Simplicity is key.

But at the same time, prioritization is important. You can have your own codes for what has to be done when, or you can use Brian Tracy's ABCDE method. If you decide to invest the time in this system, it's a good one without getting overcomplicated. A = Very Important, B = Important, C = Nice, D = Delegate, and E = Eliminate if you can. You can find out more by reading Brian's books (see my Reading and Resources list) or by exploring his website.[3]

So, on your daily list, assign the time and the order. Do any of the items need to be broken down further? For example, "tune up the yard

---

[3] Note to the reader: I have no affiliations with any of the authors or vendors that I mention in this book or in the Reading and Resources List. These are all resources that I personally found useful.

tractor" can be broken down into changing the oil, installing fresh, gapped spark plugs, and replacing the air and fuel filters. Remember me saying that the more detail you can give items, the more likely you'll be able to complete them? The more you break them down into clear tasks, the more likely you'll be to understand how long they'll take, and complete them. Before doing my lists this way, I'd get to the task "tune up the lawn tractor" and realize I hadn't ordered the filters. Then I'd add the time to go buy filters, and get discouraged because now I was behind.

Make sure you have the detail. The point here is to be thorough, but speedy. If you have to spend a lot of time on your to-do lists, you're just not going to do them.

A few other tips. Make sure you limit your main list each day to what you can realistically accomplish. If you have "tune-up the lawn tractor" AND "clean the house" and they are both at four hours each, this is too much. If you have "tune-up the lawn tractor" and six little 30-minute things, that's also too much. Other things will intrude and not everything will get done.

Build in rewards. Remember what we said about habits? Habits are circular reward systems. Build some time into your schedule where can pat yourself on the back and do something you like.

Remember to list short to-dos, like remembering to take out the trash, in their own section so they don't interfere with the other items. I put mine in a short list to the right of my main list. I recommend not starting them first unless you have to (like emails or calls). Tackle a high priority item first and then hit the mini-list. Consider getting them all done as a group and then go back to the other items.

Some of the task arrangement will depend on your day pattern DNA. Are you an early bird or a night owl? In between? Put your important tasks in blocks where your energy is highest. This is another area where compartmentalization is handy. I like to start the day at 7 am and in the hour between 7 am and 8 am, read and resolve all of my email. Whatever works for you.

The big stuff. Back to the airplane. Look at your one-year and five-year lists. Pick off the "big stuff" like the airplane you're going to build, the book you're going to write, and the trip around the world you are going to make. When it's time to begin these, spend at least half a day breaking the big dream down into manageable steps. Because these are large projects, this will also give you the opportunity to determine the resources and the timeline you'll need.

The big dreams and projects should be managed as projects and then once you get down to the day-to-day, you'll have the line-by-line info to place on your to-do lists.

Clean Up and Add-Ons
Once a month take some time to review your five-year list, your one-year list, and next month's list. Invariably things will fall off and other things will be put on. Every three or four months I redo my year list because of changes, and I prune and add to the five-year list. There's no reason why you can't start a ten-year or longer list – depending on your age and your career, you may want to have a wish list that gradually turns to reality.

Reducing Stress
The amount of stress you are feeling in any given moment is going to drive how productive and happy you are. If you're feeling overwhelmed, drop back and take stock. If it's temporary and you're on a short, energetic push to finish something, that's one thing. But if you're feeling that you're fighting a losing battle, that is another. Stop what you're doing and take a break. We're not on this planet to see how much we can accomplish. We're here to live our lives as fully as we can, in as much happiness and appreciation

as we can. Keeping things simpler rather than more complicated will help.

Fine-Tuning

Continuously improve. After you've read all three Sections, and applied the advice in the exercises, circle back here to your to-do lists and your master task lists, and ask yourself this question: "Do my short- and long-range goals, based upon my beliefs and values, sync with my day-to-day activities? Spend some quiet time thinking about this. Now is the time to correct any mismatches and improve how you're spending your time. Not be to macabre, but you don't want to reach your deathbed and suddenly say, "Oh no, that's really not the life I wanted, I wish I had . . . ."

This is not to say that you won't be always feeling that you have work to continue, things to complete, and unfulfilled dreams. That is our human condition in an imperfect world – but why not feel that you made the most of it?

Finally, to-do lists are not about time management. They are about attention and values management. Time is relative, and we can feel overwhelmed with one task or with 10.

The 80/20 Rule

Most of us learned the 80/20 Rule, also known as the Pareto Principle (economist Vilfredo Pareto was the first to postulate the rule), because the power and simplicity of the rule make it handy in decision-making.

As it applies to your choices of tasks, it says that 20 percent of what is on your list will get you 80 percent of the results for that day. This is the reason we're so selective about what we commit to doing.

Correspondingly, 80 percent of the things you work on will only give you 20 percent of the results you seek, and will consist of the little chores that often get you off track.

The lesson is to do the big 20 percent contributors first. The second lesson is to make a list of the things you're NOT going to do anymore. Hire someone else to mow the yard, change the oil in the airplane, or clean the house.

Decluttering

Speaking of making things simpler . . . throw open your closets and drawers. Is everything in its place and uncluttered? Aha, I thought so. If you answered, "Of course," then you are in the two percent of the population that has every-thing under control, all the time.

Like Parkinson's First Law, which postulates "work expands so as to fill the time available for its completion," closets are a variation of the third law, "Expansion means complexity . . . and complexity decay." Or, as I like to put it, "It doesn't matter how big or small a closet is, items will expand to fill it completely."

The Law of Clutter. Accumulation begets clutter. What is clutter? It is stuff lying around that you haven't had time to organize. Physically organizing is straightforward; don't let all the decluttering books tell you it's complicated. Where we get into trouble is with the emotional attachments to things and to habits.

The next time you are in your personal space where you live, take a look around. This might be a one-room apartment or a home. Are you using and appreciating everything you see? Are there things that you look past, thinking that you'll get to it later? You may be a person who doesn't mind clutter, or think you are. Or you may be continuously bothered by clutter, espe-cially other's people's clutter.

As you read through this book, you will real-ize that every rule I postulate depends upon you deciding to make choices about things. When you look past clutter, you're making a choice.

Our physical environment is inextricably linked with our emotional environment. When you keep looking at something that's still in your physical space, you're attached to it for a reason. For example, if you have a large collection of DVDs or CDs, or for some of us older folks, LPs (long-playing vinyl records) or tapes, and you don't listen to them, you're holding on because you want to be able to listen, even when you don't. When you keep the collection even when you doubt you will listen, or keep the clothing in the closet that you're not ever going to wear again, you're expressing an emotional attachment to the physical items that make you feel better.

Over the course of six house moves I have held onto a shoebox full of letters from the past. How often do I look at them? I never look at them. But there is something comforting knowing that I *can* look at them. In the next closet cleanup, I'll look at them one more time and toss because I realize the attachment is sentimental and it's clogging my closet. Or, maybe not.

When you recognize that your mind is driving these attachments, you may be able to step back and re-evaluate whether you really want to hold onto everything. I can't make this choice for you. But you can. Think through why you want to hold onto something. There may be another way to "hold on" to an item. Photograph it, knowing that you'll still have the memory. Then discard or give away.

Decluttering and Organizing Tricks

- ✓ Resist the temptation to put things in dark corners and closets. They will accumulate at twice the normal rate.
- ✓ Keep horizontal surfaces free of things; if you have vases, or art objects, reevaluate their placement and number periodically because they will tend to accumulate.
- ✓ Build storage vertically for bookcases and cabinets, going as high as you can. It keeps a clean and organized look.
- ✓ Have a "junk drawer" in every room. Extraneous stuff goes into it until you can't fit any more, and then you know it is time to clean it out and start again.
- ✓ Keep "stuff" out of sight with cabinet and shelf doors to hide it.
- ✓ Have at least one closet where you can throw things in and not worry about it until, like the junk drawer, it has to be sorted because things begin to bust out.

✓ Concentrate on a room at a time if you have a home; otherwise it will feel over-whelming.

✓ In any big organization push, start in the lowest portion of the home and create storage. Then go to the top floor and work down. You might need several passes to get it really neat.

If you're someone who likes to have a neat and clean space, and gets bored quickly with what you have, read "Fun and Change" below.

If you are super serious about decluttering spaces and the emotional techniques that the Japanese propose (think Marie Kondo), consider approaching it from a *"Dostadning,"* or "art of death cleaning," point of view. This is a Swedish practice of cleaning out *before* people die. If you've ever been through this sorting process after a death, you know that it can be awful. And while my suggestion to take this kind of attitude toward your own organizing may sound depress-ing, it's definitely something to think about. Im-agine having your own affairs completely in order? That's a good feeling, not a bad one.

You can even take this one step further and write your own obituary. Update it as your life proceeds, and keep all your important papers in a place, organized, where others can find them.

You may be thinking, "Why should I care? I'll be gone," but if you think hard about it, isn't there a tiny voice inside that tells you it would be a nice thing to do for others?

Digital Clutter

Finally, the elephant in the room: digital clutter. Set a schedule for dealing with this massive, easy-to-ignore subset of too much stuff. This includes:

- ✓ Old email
- ✓ The pictures trove
- ✓ Apps you no longer use
- ✓ Subscriptions you no longer need
- ✓ Old computer files
- ✓ Old digital devices you don't use

If you want to hold on to everything even though you're not using it, like the letters in the shoebox, you can simply transfer everything to a USB drive (scan) and store it safely somewhere. This is another area where people will thank you when you leave the planet.

Tricks for photographs. The longer you live, the more photos you'll have. If you're of an older generation, they will be physical photos, and if you're younger you'll have them on your computer and phone. You know you have a lot of photos when you try to find one to show your friends and you keep scrolling and scrolling and say, "Where did that one go?" Later on, you'll see it immediately and wonder why you couldn't find it.

If you're in the older generation group, you can decide to digitize your most favorite photos, or you can actually place them in frames that take an assortment of photos. It depends on how you feel about displaying them.

If you're younger, you may like the solution I settled on: a digital photo frame. You can have more than one frame in the house or at work, and it's easy to change out the collections via SD card. Get tired of a photo? Remove it from the card.

A nice middle ground: select the photos you love the most from your boxes and albums, and send them off to be digitized. Then put them into a digital frame and have some of them printed to hang up.

Fun and Change

We seek fun, change, and rewards. These are the essences of distraction. As soon as we recognize them, the better we can manage them. Our brains are wired to switch gears as soon as we perceive that there is something more exciting to do than the task at hand. This drives the social media habit: "Oh, who is calling? Will this call remove me from having to do what I am doing right now? Surely it will be more interesting." And then we take the call. Or answer the email ping. Or the text.

Recognize that we will gravitate toward change and toward fun, or things that we think will be fun. This is normal and natural. But it doesn't mean that we cannot choose what we're going to pay attention to in the moment. If we don't recognize this power, then we will be flinging ourselves at everything.

So, recognize this habit, or propensity, for fun and change, and evaluate it in the moment. Actively decide how compartmentalized you are going to be in what you are doing. I can't give you a hard and fast rule, like the TV sound, because you will need to evaluate where you are in each moment. But make sure you give yourself the power to make that decision. It's your decision.

Use fun and reward to look forward to and drive your self-discipline in each block of concentrated accomplishment. Instead of allowing distraction, you will know that at the end of this scheduled block of work you can go do something you want to do that's different from your work block. Even if we absolutely love what we're doing in a work block, at some point we will yearn for the change to something else, and the rewards that come with it.

If you opt for the fun thing in the moment, accept that and don't get mad at yourself. This just compounds the emotions and robs you of the fun. Remember acceptance?

Think back to the decluttering discussion. One really fun and interesting thing you can do if you have complete control over your physical space is to move the furniture, paint the walls, hang new things on the walls, or change the lighting. New space! It translates into fun and change. It's refreshing.

Your Physical Self

I wasn't sure if I was going to cover health in this condensed book, but decided that it's a strong contributor to life enjoyment. There are plenty of resources for you to explore if this is a problem area. Just remember to balance enough **sleep** with a healthy **diet** and adequate **exercise**. Just what you wanted to hear.

Mindfulness and Inner Peace

Happiness is not something you get. Happiness is something you already have the capacity for –

it's simply a matter of understanding it in a new light. Sam Harris, in his book, *Waking Up*, says, "Most of us spend our time seeking happiness and security without acknowledging the underlying purpose of our search. Each of us is looking for a path back to the present: We are trying to find reasons to be satisfied *now*."

Our search for happiness usually begins with thinking about the past and comparing it to the present, or thinking about the future and comparing it to the present. The actual "present" disappears as we think thoughts of the past or the future. This becomes the essence of distraction; we are not here, right now.

The practice of mindfulness tries to get us to stop and realize where we really are: We are here right now. Philosophers throughout the ages have wrestled with this concept, with Eckhart Tolle writing an entire book titled *The Power of Now*, a *New York Times* bestseller.

Mindfulness takes many forms, from meditation to prayer, to listening to "brainwave music" to hypnosis, and an assortment of apps that lead you through awareness exercises. The "now" ends up being an awareness of sensations, sights, sounds, and thoughts, appearing and fading in each moment. Language loses its ability to represent what is happening and consciousness is freed.

This book will not teach you how to meditate, or be in the "now," but I hope that it does prompt you to seek out more information, whether that is through apps or books that appear in the Reading and Resources list at the end of this book. Give some of the apps a test drive. A meditation practice of even 10 minutes a day can make a difference in your health and your happiness levels.

My own sense of mindfulness and its attendant acceptance of "what is," brings together all of the effort around the topic of distraction and disperses it. Once again in his book *Waking Up*, Sam Harris says, "It is your mind, rather than circumstances themselves, that determines the quality of your life. Your mind is the basis of everything you experience and of every contribution you make to the lives of others. Given this fact, it makes sense to train it."

Finally, Sam says, "In my view the realistic goal to be attained through spiritual practices is not some permanent state of enlightenment that admits of no further efforts but a capacity to be free in this moment, in the midst of whatever is happening. If you can do that, you have already solved most of the problems you will encounter in life."

"Stop wasting your time looking for the key to happiness...the door is open and un-locked...just walk through it."

—Steve Maraboli

Section III: How to Reach Your Dream

There are some simple facts that prevent most people from figuring out how to reach big goals — and even small goals — that seem within reach when you begin thinking about them.

Earlier in my business career I provided some coaching for CEOs of small businesses. My question to the top person in the organization was,

"What's the one thing you don't have the answer to that is keeping you up at night?"

The answer was shocking.

"I don't know what our mission is."

That's the same as saying you do not understand what the company's purpose is. Why are we in business?

If you don't know why you're in business, then you won't understand your customers or your products.

Then I asked, "What are your values?"

The CEO answered, "I haven't thought about it."

I hid my surprise as best I could, saying, "Well, let's begin there. Let's establish the company's mission, based upon its values. These are the things that your customers care deeply about."

Several of these small companies decided to go out of business, and several more decided to change their direction, based on their newly minted mission statement, becoming profitable and reaching the goals they had set.

You may not be running a business, but you are certainly running your own life. Do you have a mission statement? Are your values clear and written down? Do you know what your goals are and where you are on the plan to get there?

If you don't, don't despair. Most of us, more than 95 percent in fact, have not written down our goals.

So, complete your journey through this small book, and get started. It's never too late.[4]

Where to Start

The ideas I am about to share are my own opinions based on what has worked for me and worked for my coaching clients. The caveat is that you will need to invest a small amount of dedicated time to go through the process.

We routinely spend large blocks of time in recreation, whether it is watching TV, going to a sports event, or shopping. Yet, most people I have talked to do not have written goals.

If you decide to spend four or five hours over a weekend or two to work through my instructions, you will have a mission statement, your five top values, and your top five goals written out. You will have a timeline and a "how to get there" list for your top goal.

There are entire books written on achievement, defining your purpose, and establishing

---

[4] Reader note: What follows is a version of my goal-setting method in *Dream Take Flight*. If you've read that and gone through the entire sequence, then jump to "Pulling it All Together."

goals. This book is not meant to replace the advice and techniques that are already out there, but to assemble the best ideas and get you started. Most folks are not willing to work through an entire book to figure out their goals. While my instructions will take dedicated effort, they are a shortcut. You can decide.

Many of us fail at getting what we want because our fears overcome our willpower. We are afraid we will not get what we most want. We are afraid to dream, and we are afraid to risk what we already have. We gravitate toward comfort. To figure out what you really want, you will have to get out of your comfort zone and ask yourself some tough questions. You'll have to spend some dedicated time in soul searching.

Deciding what we want in life is Zen-like. It's muddy but clear; it's complicated but it's simple. It's hard and it's easy. It's easy because what I'm asking you to do in the first phase can be done in four hours. It's not easy because after we have figured out what we want, we have to figure out how to get it.

Here's the plan. You will spend four to six hours over two weekends to hammer this out. When you are done, you will have a plan written in your journal along with your life's mission and your core values. Marrying these two items together will give you the answer to what you want in life, and then (and only then) can we begin goal setting and then planning.

Plan on spending two to four hours on Saturday, two to three hours on Sunday, and finishing up the following weekend on Saturday or Sunday. There is no reason why you can't take longer than this, or allow more incubation time between the sessions.

Session 1: An Inner Journey

Sit down with a notebook or journal and a pen or pencil.

Answer the following questions. These are standard introspection questions that you will find in most books on goal setting and achievement. Answering them will help you discover what you care about most.

If your doctor told you that you had six months to live, in perfect health, what would you do in that time? Take as much time as you need to ponder this and write out in your notebook.

If you had all of the resources and money that you wanted, what would you do differently? You might not do anything differently but, if so, write that down in your notebook.

Finally, answer this question: What would you want others to say about you at your funeral service? Write out at least two things.

Now, let these thoughts and what you have written incubate overnight. They will percolate through your subconscious and you might be surprised at additional items that pop out in the next session.

Session 2: What You Care About

Look at your journal and read through what you wrote. Is it accurate? Is there anything else that you want to add? Go ahead and spend the time to do this.

The things that you wrote tell you about your most closely held values and principles. It is principles and values that provide the fuel or energy for your accomplishment and the pathway to your dreams.

List at least 10 values that resonate with you in your journal.

What are your values? Unless you have done this before, you may be confused. By values, I mean the noun, with a dictionary definition of:

The regard that something is held to deserve; the importance, worth, or usefulness of something.

Synonyms include, worth, usefulness, advantage, benefit, gain, profit, good, help, merit.[5]

Also:

A person's principles or standards of behavior; one's judgment of what is important in life.
Synonyms: principles, ethics, moral code, morals, standards, code of behavior.[6]

So, values are a combination of worth to us, and drive our behavior. This combination is very powerful, as we will see in a moment. Your list might look like this:

Acceptance
Accomplishment
Appreciation
Awareness
Challenge
Community
Confidence
Control
Decisiveness
Empathy

---

[5] Source: Master Writer Dictionaries (MasterWriter.com)
[6] Source: Master Writer Dictionaries (MasterWriter.com)

Energy
Friendship
Financial Security
Harmony
Humor
Humility
Imagination
Intimacy
Learning
Neatness
Optimism
Patience
Persistence
Power
Punctuality
Perfection
Reflection
Responsibility
Security
Sharing
Self-reliance
Spirituality
Teamwork
Trust
Vision
Volunteering
Wisdom

This is a fraction of what you can find in Internet lists. Take your time in picking your favorites. Make up your own.

Circle 15 values that are most important to you. Take a 15–minute break. When you return to this task, pick the top five to eight values and write these in your journal or someplace where the list will be easy to find.

Session 3: Discover Your Mission

You can continue on from the values session or let things incubate.

After reviewing your values, write a mission statement. This is your very own, private statement that you alone can see. Of course, you can share it, but right now it is yours to reflect upon. Use your top five to eight values.

Here's an example. The values may be:

Happiness
Confidence
Sharing; love
Humor
Challenge

The statement could be: "To live life in confidence and happiness, sharing my challenges with others with humor and love; to leave work of significance behind."

This exercise will help you further define your values and determine what things in life really create passion, excitement, and enthusiasm. Your dreams will materialize in front of you. If you find yourself emotional at this phase, then you are on the right track.

Some books on goal setting suggest categories for goal setting. While this is not necessary, it may provide additional structure for your goals list. Some of the categories you can use are Family, Career, Relationships, Health, Community, Recreation, Personal Growth, and Spirituality. Feel free to use these or any other categorizations that fit you.

Session 4: Find Out What You Want

In this next to last session, about two hours, you will stir values, principles, core beliefs, and wants into a mix that will produce powerful goals.

What dreams and visions materialized out of your previous sessions? Write these down.

It could be anything from a walk in the woods, a challenging climb, learning to ski or play a sport, write a book, learn photography, raise a family, write poetry, travel the world, learn to cook, retire early, perform community service, start a business, or build an airplane.

Once you've done this, rest for several days and let the ideas percolate. Your brain will work on them as you go about your day. You'll find them popping into your mind at odd times. This is a good sign.

Session 5: Planning the Dreams

You cannot do everything. In this phase you will need to evaluate the things you are doing now. Let's do that. Write down a list of *everything* you are doing in your life now. Draw a matrix or table. Start on the left with an item, then decide whether it's discretionary or not, then long-term/short-term, then rate 1-10 on whether it fits in with your values, then 1-10 on how passionate it makes you feel.

Right now, we won't worry about money (what it costs).

Now look at the non-discretionary items. Are they really required? Is there a way you could rearrange your life to not do some of these things? Think about this. It's fine if you end up not dropping any of these, but do examine them carefully. If you have high scores with these in fitting with your purpose and passion, then they should stay, of course.

On to the discretionary items. Here is where your scores really help you differentiate between items. Pick off the top 10 items and move them to a list. Reflect on the items and think about any other ways you could evaluate them. What will happen is that some of these items will jump out at you. Your emotional brain will pick out at least one and perhaps two that speak to you. Let the list incubate.

After a day of leaving your list alone, at least one of your items will grow on you. This is the time for you to sit down again in some reflective time. You will know if this is the top goal. If it is, then spend some time figuring out *how* you will achieve it. Not all of this information will appear right now, which is fine.

Write the goal down along with ideas for achievement and a timeline.

Constantly reflect on and evaluate your goals; write them in a journal and review every day. This sounds hokey, but it works.

Session 6: Six Sigma Meets the Secret

Your brain on goals – sometimes I refer to this concept as "Six Sigma Meets the Secret." Six Sigma is a rational and logical method of problem-solving using data and objective experiments to remove variation from a process, typically in a manufacturing environment. But humans do not make decisions based on logic. Humans make nearly all decisions based on emotion. Then we rationalize our decision if it does not align with the data. "I decided based on my gut feel," is a reflection of this decision-making method. We are saying, it's okay, the gut is smarter that the brain."

In fact, our emotional brain made the decision and, in the moment of that decision, the rest of our conscious resources make the case for its logic – an emotional logic. This is fine as long as we realize that this is what is happening.

So, when we choose our top goal after going through both the values analysis and the emotional "jumps out at you" review, we end up harnessing the highly powerful, emotional brain to drive accomplishment. The brain goes to work for us, and in a series of complex reviews and judgments, figures out how to get what we want.

This interplay and balance between logic and the law of attraction are crucial to an achievement plan. A cycle develops and alternates in a natural rhythm between the two of them. All of the logic in the world will not convince the subconscious mind to believe something; it is the power of emotions—the fuel, if you will—that drives achievement. Then values, belief, self-knowledge, and the data have to be lined up in the same direction to produce the spark and then the ignition of your deepest passion.

Values drive beliefs; beliefs drive emotions; emotions drive goals; goals drive achievement.

What to do next: Take about an hour to review your work in your journal. If you see any disconnects, think them through. Review your top five goals and decide which one you will pursue. If you've followed the directions, you will find a powerful magnet drawing you in.

Pick one to begin. You've done enough work to know that the five goals are achievable and ignite excitement. Now what you will do is figure out how to get what you want.

Ask yourself, "What do you need to do to reach the first goal on your list?"

List out what things have to be accomplished.

Ask yourself, "What other things must I give up to get what I want?"

List these items.

Pull out or print out a long-range calendar. List the subtasks you'll need to accomplish and put them into the calendar. Important: The dates are mileposts. They are flexible. Your brain will reject hard and fast dates. Your passion and excitement will drive task completion.

Session 7: Happiness and Stress

The following tips can make a difference in how fast you reach your goals.

Attitude. Think about what you want, not about what you don't want. Sometimes this is not easy, but developing goal-setting habits will help. It's fine to be realistic, but never allow yourself to fall into negativity. It will only impede your progress.

Personal Power. You have the power to decide how you will react to life events. I was well into my thirties before I realized this fact, and when I saw it, an entirely new world opened up for me. Because of the range of human personality types, this basic and important principle may not be evident to everyone. Those who have not discovered it yet tend to blame misfortune on others instead of taking action to create positive and transformative responses to view events with a different perspective.

This personal power will allow you to control and enjoy your own life with great enthusiasm. In accepting personal responsibility for where you are and what you are doing, you will find that your world opens up to others.

Stress is energy. "Being stressed" is thought of as bad. If we think it is bad, then it IS bad, and

79

the effects will manifest as fatigue, impatience, avoidance, and unhappiness. Knowing that you have the power to view life events through your very own filter, why not view stress as positive energy?

Acceptance. Accept the situation you are in fully and allow the energy to fuel your own awareness and patience. Over time this habit will drive positive mental and bodily responses to pressure and help you stay focused and positive. The more open-minded we are to our ability to do this, the better it will work.

Habits. In Section I, I talked about the power of habits. Habits guide everything we do. Our brains are wired into habits with specific rewards and reinforcements. We go through each day rarely thinking about habits. But changing our habits can be a powerful way to getting more of what we want and less of what we don't want.

Return to the exercise you did on page 9 under Habits. How far did you get? Pick up where you left off by picking another habit you want to change. Write down ways you could change your unwanted habit or install the new one. Reward yourself every time you succeed. Go one at a time so that it is not overwhelming.

Give Some Time Away. By now you are thinking about every opportunity to work on and enjoy your goal. Your brain is figuring out how to create more time to achieve the steps necessary to achieve your biggest dream. Your planner is full. "I wish I had some time," you say to yourself. If you're like me, you are crowbar-ring every moment you can in to get things done.

Although counterintuitive, the best way to find time is to share and give time. Get out of your goal zone now and then and spend time with others in some capacity. Volunteer, teach, visit someone, or invite others to see your projects.

Sharing yourself with others from time to time opens up your own perspective and will drive creativity and a renewed enjoyment of your own goals.

"You have to decide what your highest priorities are and have the courage—pleasantly, smilingly, non-apologetically, to say "no" to other things. And the way you do that is by having a bigger "yes" burning inside."

—Stephen R. Covey

Goal-Setting Myths

You now know that achieving a dream does not start with goals. To reinforce the concept, here are the central misconceptions of goal setting.

Conventional wisdom in the goal-setting arena is very clear: goals should be brainstormed, prioritized, time bound, written down, and adhered to rigorously or we won't achieve them.

Not so.

In my experience, using these principles without an intelligent framework dooms us to failure and disappointment. It is no wonder that so many people have an aversion to the phrase "goal setting" or "New Year's Resolutions." These feelings come from repeated failures in trying to get a goal system to work for us. We would rather not think about it and skim along hoping that we will get some of what we want in life and not have to deal with the process.

As a result, most people do not achieve the level of happiness, satisfaction, and pleasure that they could otherwise have in their personal lives and in their careers and businesses. Understanding the myths of goal setting is the first step in learning how to discover the power and ease of goal achievement.

Myth #1: Start your goal setting by brainstorming a list of things to work on (goals)
No. This idea presupposes that you already know what you should be working on. Most people do not have a good understanding of themselves and their motivations, much less their goals in life. Nearly 95 percent of the population cannot succinctly answer the question "What do you want out of life?"

If we cannot answer this question, and we do not know what we want, how can we set life goals? There is certainly a place for brainstorming in the goal-setting process, but it is not at the beginning. Without alignment between self-knowledge, beliefs and values, and your passions, your subconscious mind will reject most efforts at goal setting.

Myth #2: All goals must be time bound

No. Desperation and depression follow from putting dates on goals and then not meeting them. What is the worst thing that could happen? There are goals that have dates and must be accomplished (buy gas for the car), however, goal setting is more complicated than this, and without constant adjusting of deadlines, if you have deadlines at all, our minds will not embrace them.

While we can spend time looking at the long-range picture of what we want in life, we have to be flexible in assigning timeframes. An example would be "getting fit." Does this have an end goal? Yes, and it has interim goals, but it's a moving target. If we get sick and interrupt our schedule, are we failures because we did not reach the interim goal? No, because we adjust the times out to accommodate circumstances. To be rigid about deadlines will damage self-esteem and produce discouragement and fatigue. This is a major contributor to stress and the feeling of overload, especially in the workplace. Self-esteem and confidence are critical to achievement, balance, and happiness.

Myth #3: "Just Do It"

This is a fun saying that Nike invented, and it's been used everywhere to mean anything and everything . . . but in the goal-setting arena, what does this tell us? It tells us to just pick something and then pursue it, no matter what.

No.

While it is not a bad thing to pursue something important with passion and energy, to be spending all that energy on something that is not going to get you where you want to go will be a waste of time. The supposition here is that we simply settle on something, and go for it. In *Alice In Wonderland*, Alice finds the Cheshire Cat perched up in a tree.

"Oh Puss, could you please tell me which way to go?" asks Alice.

"Well, that depends on where you want to get to," says the cat.

"Oh, it really doesn't matter, as long as I get somewhere," says Alice.

"Then it really doesn't matter which way you go!" says the cat.

The point here is if we have not figured out the best route, if we don't have a map, and we run off in any direction, we may end up in a place where we do not want to be.

Myth #4: Always prioritize your goals

No. Prioritization is used when brainstorming multiple goals, not after they are established. Prioritize what you are going to do *right now*, in this moment. Change is always going on around us, and we must have the flexibility in our schedule and in our stance to be able to respond to changing circumstances.

Myth #5: Stick to your goals and don't quit

No. Again, the hallmark of our world is change. If the underlying reasons for a certain goal change, you must adjust appropriately to that change. This is tough psychologically, as we normally hold on to stable environments and resist any changes. But doing this will really hold us back.

As for quitting, quitting can be a terrific strategy to get off the wrong track and on to the right one. There's a little book that you might have seen or heard about called, *The Dip* by Seth Godin that tells us quitting can be the best thing we can do if it gets us unstuck and onto a track where we can be the best at something – realizing and pursuing our passion.

Myth #6: Share your goals with your family and friends so that you are committed to achieving them.

No. And, it's fine if you disagree.

Self-esteem is critically important to the goal-setting process and all you need are your friends telling you that you are a fool, a dreamer, "'round the bend" or plain crazy. This isn't to say you shouldn't share an important goal with a loved one or close friend, just be judicious about it. You're not doing this exercise for your friends; you are doing this for yourself.

The time to be secretive is in the beginning, as your plan emerges. Protect your ideas and excitement until you are clear about your journey. Be ready for ridicule and criticism, outright as well as veiled, when it arrives. This will give you conviction and strength of purpose. I spent months planning my airplane purchase before letting anyone know – and then easily endured "You must be crazy" and "What are you thinking?"

Your passion is first a secret passion . . . and then there will be time to share it.

Myth #7: Goal setting should be done in a logical way so that your emotions don't steer you in the wrong direction.

No. If your logical mind comes up with your goals plan, but your emotional brain, or heart, if you will, does not "like" the plan, then it will NEVER happen. I see this all the time at the end of the year when people set the goals that they "should" do . . . they "should" lose weight, stop smoking, save more money. We know that the results are usually less than what we hoped for. Without alignment between our inner beliefs and our goals, we just can't get traction for accomplishment.

Myth #8: A goal plan should drive project plans that are detailed, written down, and worked on every day.

Don't make it complicated. Do the up-front work. Once you understand that your goals have to be aligned with your values, your beliefs, and your passions, you can put the process on auto-pilot and find that things are being delivered to you. This is an important concoction of logic and emotion – establish the logic, allow the emotional alignment, and watch the Universe deliver what you want. Once you get good at the process, you no longer have to do the paperwork, so to speak, to get the deliveries.

Summary

You have probably seen the acronym for goal setting, called "SMART."

S = Specific
M = Measurable
A = Attainable
R = Realistic
T = Time bound or Timely

One of the reasons I don't like acronyms is that someone made them up to be clever, and maybe the capital letters don't really do a good job of saying what the formula is. Let's look at this one.

S is okay for Specific. Your goals *should* be as specific as possible.

M is okay for Measurable, we should be able to measure our goals.

A for Attainable is redundant; why would we even list a goal if we did not think it was attainable? Let's replace this with Aligned Action. We know that if our goals are not aligned with our values and beliefs, we will not take action on it. The goal must be aligned.

R for Realistic is redundant once again. If the goal was *not* realistic (in our own mind) we would not be attempting it, and many big goals are *not* realistic at the outset. Let's replace this with Reinforcing. If our goals are reinforced by our values and beliefs, then we can achieve them.

And lastly, **T**, for Timely. We already said that most goals should not have a specific hard and fast date assigned to them. So this won't work. Let's replace Timely with Tempting. If your goal is not tempting, if it is not interesting, fun, and something to look forward to, you won't do it, will you? So we now have:

S = Specific
M = Measurable
A = Aligned Action
R = Reinforcing (values)
T = Tempting

Realize that accomplishing some of the tasks in your plan will require you to give up other things. Don't let this discourage you, and stay focused on your goals. Your brain will work in tandem with your emotions to drive you to completion.

Your mind and all of the resources available to it are working in concert to accomplish your goal. You **will** achieve your goal, and it will bring lasting joy and self-confidence.

Congratulations. You are now one of less than 5 percent of the human population with a values list, mission statement, and written goals with a plan to achieve them. You know where you are going and how to get there. The dreams of the world are now yours.

"Let our advance worrying become advance thinking and planning."

—Winston Churchill

Pulling it All Together

O nce you've established your values and then your goals, loop back around and read the section on the power of choice principles once more. This will help your subconscious mind embrace the techniques. Then decide which of the "rules" would help you the most in getting the time and attention you need to work toward the things you want.

The "power of the Post-Its" reveals itself in flexible and reflective planning — not cast in stone — but thinking on paper that can be moved around to accommodate change. Don't allow your planning and to-do systems to get too complicated or you will not always have the discipline to adhere to them. Build it into your schedule.

There are going to be bumps in the road that upset your plans. Learning how to deal with these constructively and get back to what's important to you will take some of the stress of change and uncertainty out of the equation.

To get the most out of this book, keep looping back to the principles and then take up another rule in Section II. After a few reads, you'll find yourself much more productive, less stressed, and happier.

Pay particular attention to the section Mindfulness and Inner Peace. Your mind and your thinking determine the quality of your life. The more you master the power of conscious awareness, the more profound each moment of your life will become.

I'll leave you with five summary tips based on what you've read in this book.

✓ **Learn to compartmentalize.** We talked about some techniques to do this in Section II Tips & Tricks. Compartmentalizing is a form of protecting yourself, but still uses situational awareness where you balance concentration with awareness. As you get better at it, you'll experience fewer distractions and more focus.

✓ **Don't forget your power of choice.** In each moment you can decide how you will react to a situation. You may not be able to change what is happening, but you can change how you respond to it.

✓ **Set goals and priorities based upon your values.** These are the things that are deeply important to you. Your values will drive your attention; your attention will drive your time management.

✓ **Use tools** such as meditation/prayer, and affirmations/hypnosis to improve your ability to handle stress, employ self-discipline, discover the things you love, and work on what matters most to you.

✓ **Keep a journal**, a diary, or periodic notes. You never know when a great idea will form through your creative thoughts and produce a work of art, a book, or an amazing project or plan.

BONUS:
The Big Career
Secret

Here's a secret I'll share with you that didn't fit neatly into the other categories, but can mean a 15 to 25 percent improvement in your work life productivity, and also boost what you are paid. If you work for someone else, this is a sure-fire way to get recognized.

Here's the trick.

Most organizations do performance reviews once a year. Most organizations also tell employees what they are supposed to be doing — goals and objectives — once a year. Both employees and managers hate the process and avoid it until the last minute. I have worked in some organizations that hated it so much they just didn't do it at all. The result? Poor business performance. If employees don't know what to do or how they are measured, the entire company's productivity will be lousy.

This year — begin now — dig out your job description and goals and objectives. Don't have them? Can't find them? Go to the Human Resources (HR) Department and ask for them. HR will go into your file and find a copy from last year. No one has anything? No problem. Keep following these instructions.

If there isn't anything, then you are going to make your own. Yes, that's right – you're going to write your own job description and goals and objectives. This may take you some time, but believe me, it's important. Do a rough draft.

If you already have your job description and your goals and objectives, great. Review them. Is there anything missing? Add it.

Now write down what you've accomplished against your objectives. Be as detailed as you can, adding any return on investment (ROI) that you can think of. The best place to find ROI is in cost savings and cost avoidance. Nearly all jobs can be quantified this way; you just need to think it through. If you can show your boss that you saved the company more money than they spent on your salary and benefits, you are really on your way.

Next, make an appointment to meet with your supervisor or manager. This is the tough part, because they won't understand why you want to meet with them. Tell them you'd like to "provide an update." They will begin to worry, and think you're going to ask for a raise or quit.

When you get to their office, or other private area, close the door. Now your supervisor is really going to worry. Pull out your performance update, and say, "I just wanted to update you on what I'm doing and make sure we're on the same page. Is there anything else I should be working on?" Hand them your accomplishments.

Your supervisor will breathe a huge sigh of relief. He or she has been spared the pain of replacing you, having to listen to a complaint, or having to reject a raise request. He or she now also has the answers and information for your performance review later in the year. Watch them smile as they read your report. Listen to them, writing down anything they say or additions or comments they have. Then thank them and leave.

That's the first step. The second part of this process is for you to update your description, and goals and objectives, and then keep track of your accomplishments. Shortly before your review, update your information, and give it to your supervisor in a folder. This process alone will raise your own productivity on the job, because you'll understand what the most important things are to be working on, and what is most important to your boss.

And if you really want to make your supervisor happy, do a self-review using your accomplishments and ROI numbers, leaving out the ratings. When your supervisor does your review, they'll use your wording. Supervisors and managers are very busy people and anything that you can do to make their job easier will not only be appreciated, it will be rewarded with better review ratings, and the opportunity for more compensation and career progression.

The lesson here is that relationship is as important as actual work performance, and that finding out and doing the things your organization needs most will improve not only your own productivity but also the success of the company.

Your Simplest Life

Reading & Resources

Clear, James. 2018. *Atomic Habits: An Easy & Proven Way to Build Good Habits & Break Bad Ones.* Avery, New York, NY.

Goldman, Daniel. 2005. *Emotional Intelligence: Why It Can Matter More than IQ.* Bantam Dell, New York, NY.

Harrari, Yuval. 2018. *Sapiens: A Brief History of Mankind.* Harper Perennial. New York, NY.

Harris, Bill. 2015. *The New Science of Super Awareness.* Centerpointe Research Institute, Beaverton, Oregon.

Harris, Bill. 2007. *Nine Principles for Conscious Living.* Centerpointe Research Institute, Beaverton, Oregon.

Harris, Russ. 2008. *The Happiness Trap: How to Stop Struggling and Start Living.* Trumpeter, Boulder, Co.

Harris, Sam. 2015. *Waking Up: A Guide to Spirituality Without Religion.* Simon & Schuster, New York, NY.

Hayes, Steven C. 2000. *Get Out of Your Mind and into Your Life.* New Harbinger Publications, Oakland, CA.

Tracy, Brian. 2017. *Eat That Frog! 21 Great Ways to Stop Procrastinating and Get More Done in Less Time.* Third Edition. Berrett-Koehler Publishers. Oakland, CA.

Tracy, Brian. 2011. *No Excuses! The Power of Self-Discipline.* Da Capo Press, Philadelphia, PA.

Tracy, Brian. 2018. *The Ultimate Brian Tracy Library.* Audiobook. Nightingale-Conant. Oakland, CA.

Tolle, Eckhart. 2004. *The Power of Now: A Guide to Spiritual Enlightenment.* New World Library, Novato, CA.

Tolle, Eckhart. 2006. *A New Earth: Awakening to Your Life's Purpose.* Penguin Books, London, UK.

Web Links:

Hypnosis Programs
Rick Smith, HPD, DHyp
Certified Clinical Hypnotherapist, London UK
https://www.ricksmithhypnosis.com

Brain Entrainment and Meditation
Centerpointe Research Institute
1600 NW 167th Pl Ste 320
Beaverton, Oregon 97006-4806
https://www.centerpointe.com

LISA TURNER

A certified Lean Institute Black Belt in business productivity with a doctorate in Management Science, Turner is more than qualified to advise both businesses and individuals on how to get the most out of a day's work or play.

In *Team Steps Guide to Problem Solving,* her first business management book (2015, Turner

Creek), Lisa reveals the shortcuts that work to solve problems on the production floor – and in life itself. In her career as a manufacturing engineer, Lisa saved thousands of dollars that were being spent unnecessarily by eliminating waste in the manufacturing process.

Two years later, in *House Keys – The Essential Homeowner's Guide* (2017, Turner Creek), Lisa took her principles into the area of home inspection. In her career as a home inspector and general contractor, she discovered and wrote about all the things that builders were missing or doing wrong in home construction. She's saving homeowners thousands of dollars now by revealing the tips and tricks to get a great home built for a small price, and time and money saving tricks on home maintenance and home organization. She writes the home improvement column for the *Clay County Progress* newspaper in her hometown of Hayesville, North Carolina.

Switching gears, Lisa decided to write her own story – an adventure memoir – in *Dream Take Flight* (2019, Turner Creek). In this inspiring story, Lisa "breaks the rules" for women in the 1970s, working high-rise construction and starting a bicycle shop. She goes on to build an airplane in her garage, flying the small airplane from Florida to Maine and back and reconciles with her family in the process.

The theme that runs through Lisa Turner's life is one of high achievement born of the ability to choose the most important things to work on. At the end of her memoir is a goal setting section that high schools are now using to help students discover values and set goals that are achievable and meaningful.

In her latest book, *Your Simplest Life*, you can learn the secrets that Lisa uses to "get things done" and make sure they are the right things that bring happiness and joy to life every single day.

Visit Lisa's Author Page:

Scan to Author Page

Notes

Workbook Link

https://lisaturner.godaddysites.com/simplest-workbook